BRITAIN IN OLD PH

STREATHAM
A SECOND SELECTION

PATRICK LOOBEY &

JOHN W. BROWN

SUTTON PUBLISHING LIMITED

Sutton Publishing Limited
Phoenix Mill · Thrupp · Stroud
Gloucestershire · GL5 2BU

First published 1996

Copyright © P.J. Loobey (pictures)
          J.W. Brown (text)

British Library Cataloguing in Publication Data
A catalogue record for this book is available from the
British Library.

ISBN 0-7509-1123-9

Typeset in 10/12 Perpetua.
Typesetting and origination by
Sutton Publishing Limited.
Printed in Great Britain by
Ebenezer Baylis, Worcester.

PATRICK LOOBEY, born in 1947, has lived in Balham, Putney, Southfields and Streatham – all within the Borough of Wandsworth. He joined the Wandsworth Historical Society (founded 1953) in 1969 and has served on its archaeological, publishing and management committees, being chairman of the society from 1991 to 1994. Having collected Edwardian postcards of Wandsworth Borough and the surrounding district for more than twenty years, he has a wide-ranging collection (20,000 cards plus) encompassing many local roads and subjects.

This book complements recent titles by him covering the Borough of Wandsworth, i.e. *Streatham* (1993), *Battersea and Clapham* (1994), *Balham and Tooting* (1994), *Wandsworth* (1994 & 1996), and *Putney* (1996).

Reproductions of the views in this book are available from Patrick Loobey, 231 Mitcham Lane, Streatham, London, SW16 6PY (Tel: 0181-769 0072)

JOHN W. BROWN has lived in Streatham all his life. His family has a long association with the area dating from the 1880s, when his great grandfather, John Brown, moved to what was then a semi-rural country town on the outskirts of London.

His interest in local history was aroused when researching his family tree, in response to pleas for help from relatives in America, who were keen to learn about their roots in the UK. His fascination with the subject was encouraged by his father, Leslie Brown, who, when recalling his childhood adventures in the area at the time of the First World War, spoke of a locality which bore little resemblance to the Streatham of today.

John has written numerous books on the history of Streatham and the surrounding area, including the first volume of *Streatham in Old Photographs* which was published in 1993, and *Balham and Tooting in Old Photographs* in 1994. He publishes local history books and reprints of classic histories of the region written in the eighteenth and nineteenth centuries. He is a member of the Committee of the Local History Group of the Streatham Society, and belongs to numerous other organisations including the London Topographical Society and the Lambeth and Southwark Archaeological Society. He regularly gives talks on the history of Streatham and the surrounding area and contributes articles to various journals and publications.

Photograph credits: John Brown, pages 11, 23L, 24, 70, 73T, 87T, 97L, 98, 109L. All other photographs are from Patrick Loobey's collection.

CONTENTS

Introduction   5

1. South Streatham – The High Road   7

2. South Streatham Streets   21

3. Streatham Common & the Rookery   35

4. Central Streatham – The High Road from Streatham Station to   43
   St Leonard's Church

5. Streatham Village   53

6. Mitcham Lane   59

7. West Streatham Streets   71

8. Central Streatham – The High Road from St Leonard's Church to   85
   Streatham Hill

9. Central Streatham Streets   99

10. Streatham Hill   105

11. Streatham Hill Streets   113

Streatham High Road
looking down the dip,
c. 1900.

The Dyce fountain and Church of the English Martyrs, *c.* 1908.

INTRODUCTION

This further selection of *Streatham in Old Photographs* provides me with the wonderful opportunity to have a second bite of the cherry and present many magnificent views of the area that Pat Loobey and I were unable to include in our first book.

Limited space makes it only possible to give brief captions to each photograph and therefore wherever possible I have tried not to duplicate the information contained in our earlier volume. I have also selected views of a large number of Streatham's residential roads that were not included in our first publication so as to provide the widest possible coverage of the area. Because of the wealth of old picture postcards held in Pat Loobey's collection, my problem has been more one of what views to leave out rather than what to include.

As you turn the pages of this book I hope you will enjoy your stroll through the streets of Streatham as they were in the halcyon days of Edwardian England. Although many of the area's old buildings have long since been demolished, either at the hands of the developer or the Third Reich, much still remains to remind us of the charm of the semi-rural suburb that was Streatham in the years leading up to the First World War.

In the 230 plus photographs featured in this collection we can glimpse the wealthy inhabitants of the parish being driven in open carriages by their grooms; young ladies shielding themselves from the sun with their lace parasols; youngsters gathering on a street corner waiting their turn on a pair of stilts; and children in their sailor suits and straw hats sailing boats on the village pond or picking blackberries at the top of Streatham Common.

The local lock-up, pubs, blacksmith's forge and village green are all depicted in a series of delightful sketches by the local artist, Holland Tringham. These portray scenes of the locality little changed from the time when Dr Johnson stayed here as the house guest of Henry and Hester Thrale, or when the Prince Regent paused in Streatham while en route to Brighton, to quench his thirst and watch the cock-fighting at the Horse and Groom.

I hope this second selection of old photographs has whetted your appetite to learn more about the history of the area. All those who are interested in discovering more about Streatham's fascinating past are warmly invited to come along to the meetings of the Local History Group of the Streatham Society. These are held at 8 p.m. on the first Monday of each month in St Leonard's Church Hall in Tooting Bec Gardens, Streatham.

Since the publication of our first book, and our companion volume covering Tooting and Balham, I have received many letters from readers telling me of their memories of Streatham in days past. These have provided a valuable insight into the history of our suburb as well as a wealth of information, now preserved for future generations, which otherwise would probably have been lost for all time.

It has also brought to light some wonderful old photographs of the area which have never

been seen before outside the family albums from which they have been taken. Some of these
pictures are featured in this collection and have come to the pages of this book from as far afield
as Canada and Australia.

I would like to extend my thanks to members of the Local History Group of the Streatham
Society for their help in preparing this volume, particularly to Bob Jenner for details concerning
damage caused in Streatham by enemy action during the Second World War and to Kevin Kelly
for the sporting facts.

Special mention must also be made of the invaluable assistance provided by my brother,
Maurice, without whose continual support and collaboration this book would not have been
possible.

I would be most interested to hear from readers and I hope that this second compilation of
views will help jog memories and encourage past residents to recall their family experiences of
the area as well as to dig out their old snaps of Streatham.

John W. Brown
316 Green Lane
Streatham
London SW16 3AS

Streatham High Road by The White Lion public house, *c.* 1908.

SOUTH STREATHAM
– THE HIGH ROAD

King William IV public house. The Union Jack flutters over the newly rebuilt King William IV in 1903.
The name of the then publican, Henry Arthur Mayes, is proudly displayed over the first floor windows. He
hosted a special house-warming dinner for sixty guests in July 1903 to celebrate the opening of his new
premises. Situated at the junction of Streatham High Road and Hermitage Lane, the King William IV was
the first tavern the traveller encountered as he entered Streatham parish on the road from Croydon. A pub
has occupied this spot since at least the 1680s, trading under a number of different names over the centuries
including the Green Man, the King's Head, the Blackboy, and
the Princes Head (see page 10).

Station Parade, Norbury, c. 1902. The row of Edwardian shops flanking the western side of the London Road was erected in 1902. It begins at the railway bridge by Norbury station and ends at the River Graveney, which marks the parish boundary between Croydon and Streatham. From 1902 there was a tram terminus at Hermitage Bridge where the Croydon and London County Council (LCC) tramways met.

Norbury and Streatham tram terminus, c. 1905. The northern end of the parade of shops on the left of this picture was destroyed by a V1 flying bomb in the Second World War. On the Streatham side of Hermitage Bridge can be seen the open area of land on which the Sussex public house was erected in 1937, which survives today as the Brass Farthing. The houses to the north of the site were originally known as St George's Villas.

Death Bend 1950. A tram car trundles round 'death bend', a notorious stretch of Streatham High Road, between the King William IV public house and Hermitage Bridge, where a number of fatal accidents have taken place. One of the most tragic occurred here in October 1969 when three young men were killed and a nineteen-year-old girl was seriously injured when their Ford Zephyr skidded and crashed into the lamp post at the corner of the bend. The site now occupied by R.B. Motors can be seen on the left, at the time still undeveloped following bomb damage on 2 November 1940. The lower photograph shows the bend in 1909, when Charles Norrington baked bread in his bake house at the rear of his premises on the left of the picture. Next door William Branson advertises, on a hoarding above his depot, the delivery of London and suburban parcels on a hoarding above his depot.

King William IV public house, *c.* 1910 (see page 7). In the late eighteenth and early nineteenth century the pub standing on this site, then known as the Princes Head, had a reputation as being the haunt of highwaymen. In 1817 the publican had his licence withdrawn when it was discovered that robbers were using his blacksmith shop to melt down their ill-gotten gains. However the licence was reinstated in 1856 when the inn reopened under the new name of the King William IV.

Coulthurst Hill, 1909. For most of the nineteenth century this stretch of Streatham High Road, between the King William IV and Guildersfield Road, was known as Coulthurst Hill. It was named after the Coulthurst family who resided in Streatham Lodge, a large mansion that stood in its own grounds on the eastern side of the road. The three detached houses in the centre of this picture were known as Hereford, Bedford and Surrey Villas, and were destroyed by enemy bombing on 10 May 1941.

Bassett's Yard, 492 Streatham High Road, *c.* 1899. William Bassett and his sons ran their building business from this house until it was sold in April 1899, following William's death. Members of the Bassett family resided at 90 Lewin Road until 1994 when William's daughter, Hilda, died. At the rear of the yard, opposite the old workshops, were four small cottages, behind which can be seen the old Immanuel Church School building that stood in Factory Square.

Cow Industrial Polymers, *c.* 1980. Bassett's house can be seen on the left of the central section of Cow's offices after it had been acquired by the company and converted for commercial use. At the rear of these buildings the first purpose-built textile factory in London was erected in 1820, when Stephen Wilson constructed a silk mill here. This survives today as the coffee shop in Sainsbury's supermarket which now occupies the P.B. Cow site. For over a century Cow's produced a range of rubber goods here including the famous 'LiLo' inflatable air bed.

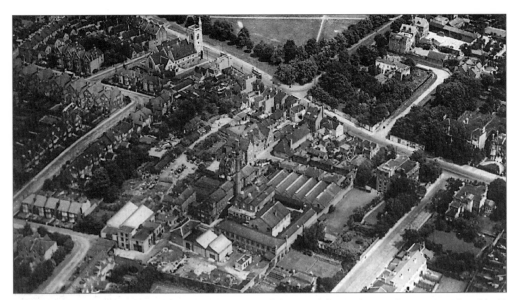

P.B. Cow's factory complex can be seen in the centre of this aerial view taken in about 1924. The old silk mill building is located to the left of the factory chimney with Immanuel Church also to the left at the top of the photograph. Occupying the site at the junction of the High Road and Streatham Common South is Streatham Court, a large mansion in which Stephen Wilson lived (see page 11). These grounds were later developed as Voss Court.

Church Place and Immanuel Church, 1914. Among this row of ancient cottages was the old Dewdrop beer shop. This was closed by the Revd Stenton Eardley shortly after he came to Immanuel Church in 1854. He was a staunch supporter of the temperance movement and felt that the Dewdrop was a bad influence on the poor in his parish. It was his zeal that led to the building of the nearby Beehive Coffee Tavern, adjacent to the Pied Bull public house, in the hope that men would prefer 'the cup that cheers' to a pint of bitter. The Beehive survives today as a solicitors office by the High Road entrance to Sainsbury's supermarket, while people continue to quench their thirst next door at the Pied Bull as they have done for more than 250 years.

Immanuel Church. Fifty years separate these two views of Immanuel Church. The upper picture shows the church shortly after it was built in 1854. It proved far too small to accommodate the rapidly growing population of South Streatham and the building seen in the lower view was erected in 1865. The 1865 church was designed by Benjamin Ferrey, FSA. As the inhabitants of the parish continued to increase in number the church was extended. In 1876 a side chapel was added at a cost of £800 and the seating capacity of the church was increased to accommodate upwards of 1,100 persons. All that remains today of the 1865 church is the tower from the top of which one can still obtain a magnificent view of the surrounding area. Note the surviving trees by the pond at the bottom of Streatham Common.

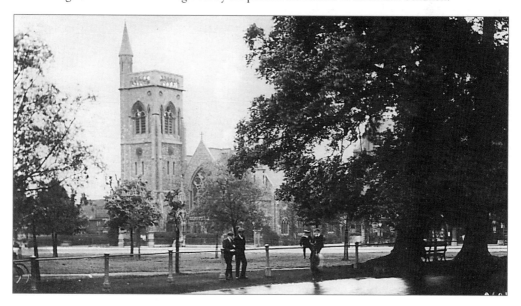

Immanuel Church, 1908.

Immanuel Church, 1908. In 1987 the body of the church was demolished and a new church was built behind the tower. The remainder of the site was developed with sheltered accommodation for the elderly and called St John's House. This was named after the college of Immanuel's first vicar, the Revd Stenton Eardley, who graduated from St John's College, Cambridge, in 1846 (see page 74). He was much loved by his parishioners and when he died in 1883, after twenty-nine years at Immanuel, twenty carriages and over 200 persons on foot followed his coffin to its final resting place at West Norwood Cemetery. The brass lectern, seen below, was presented to the church by Sir Kingsmill and Lady Key, who resided at the Rookery, a large mansion that stood at the top of Streatham Common (see page 42). Sir Kingsmill's father was twice Lord Mayor of London and his son was captain of Surrey County Cricket Club from 1894–99.

Bank Parade, Nos 426–450 Streatham High Road, *c.* 1903. For many years Bank Parade was regarded as South Streatham's premier shopping centre, with many of the area's leading traders operating from these buildings. Notable among them was Thomas Edwin Park, a butcher, whose name can be clearly seen on the glass canopy above his shop. Mr Park was a keen collector of landscape pictures, amassing a collection of more than 150 works, most by the local artist Holland Tringham (see page 97).

From No. 444 Streatham High Road a small dairy business was established by the Chalkley brothers in the early years of the twentieth century. This enterprise continued through the endeavours of a number of subsequent owners until it was eventually acquired by Curtis Brothers (see page 56) after the First World War. This picture shows one of the milkmen who operated from this dairy in the early 1900s.

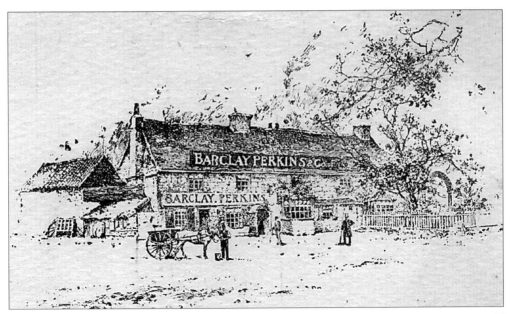

The Greyhound. The above drawing by local artist Holland Tringham (see page 97) shows the old Greyhound Inn, *c.* 1867. This was a long, low building probably built in 1730 to replace an earlier tavern of the same name. During the time of the Napoleonic Wars the Streatham Militia gathered here for refreshment before drilling and musket practice on Streatham Common. The Greyhound was also a popular stop for parish officials and at a 'visitation' here in 1769 the party enjoyed a sumptuous feast of beef, fowls, bacon and bread and butter, all washed down with wine, porter and beer, followed by tobacco all round. More humble fare was provided in 1829 when those 'beating the bounds' of the parish refreshed themselves here with nine gallons of porter valued at 15*s.* and as much bread and cheese as they could eat. The picture below, taken in 1916, shows the new pub erected on the site in 1871 by Edwin Janes. The pub was rebuilt again in 1930.

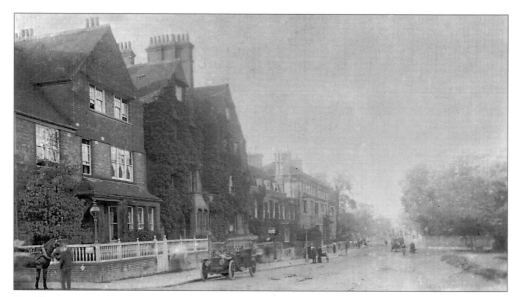

Hambly Mansions, 1908. Potter Perrin's bathroom and kitchen fittings shop now occupies the ground floor of Hambly Mansions which stands at the High Road junction with Barrow Road. The building was erected in 1877 to provide comfortable accommodation for P.B. Cow, owner of the nearby rubber factory (see pages 11 and 12). The house was built on the site of Hambly House Academy, a popular school for the sons of the gentry which was established here in 1776.

Streatham Congregational Church, 1918. A large house called Heathfield stood on this site until it was demolished in March 1900 to make way for the building of the Congregational Church which was opened for worship on 11 June 1901. Next to the church can be seen the nursery garden operated by D.T. Drysdall, the local agent for 'One & All seeds and fertilisers'. The Streatham ice rink now occupies the nursery site.

Coventry Hall, *c.* 1900. Coventry Hall was built by Lord Deerhurst, later the 7th Earl Coventry, on the site of the old Streatham manor house, the grounds of which are now occupied by Albert Carr Gardens. The origins of Coventry Hall are unclear. Accounts from James Wyatt dated 1803–4 exist 'for designing, superintending and directing the works executed at Streatham' for £5,049 16*s.* 11*d.* However, other papers dated 1811–14 refer to a house designed by John Nash and include a reference to taking down an existing building and erecting a new house for the sum of £5,750. It is not clear if the 'existing building' was the old manor house or a different building erected by Wyatt in 1803–4. Lord Deerhurst incorporated into his new home the large mahogany doors and Adams fireplaces that were formerly in his town house in Piccadilly. Coventry Hall was acquired by the Order of the Religious of St Andrew in 1894 who established a school here. After the Second World War Wandsworth Council converted the building into flats. The Hall was demolished in 1980 and a block of twenty-four houses for retired people were erected on the site in 1995. These were named Coventry Hall in memory of the Earl of Coventry's old home.

The High Road entrance to Streatham station, to the left of the tram, c. 1950. When the station was originally built in 1868 its entrance was by a small country lane leading off Streatham High Road. This survives today as Station Approach by the side of Safeways supermarket. The High Road entrance to the station probably dates from 1898 when major rebuilding work was undertaken on what was then known as Streatham Central Railway station. In 1905 the body of William Montier, of Vant Road in Tooting, was found hanging from the lamppost outside the station. Fortunately he was discovered by a local policeman, Sgt. Pascoe, who, after twenty minutes of resuscitation, miraculously managed to bring the corpse back to life. The bottom picture shows the station staff on the 'up' platform, c. 1908.

SOUTH STREATHAM STREETS

Ellison Road, c. 1912. This road is named after the Ellison family who were large landowners in South Streatham in the eighteenth century and whose property descended through many generations to form the Crooke, Ellison and Bates Estate which survived into the twentieth century (see page 74). Ellison Road is one of the few streets in south Streatham to contain almost a complete example of the different types of suburban residential buildings to be found in the area. These range from small Victorian terraced cottages at the southern end of the road to some large detached properties by Kempshott Road. Inbetween are examples of 1920s and '30s housing, together with small developments of more modern dwellings, can be found in between, including the recent erection of 1990s housing in Rama Close, opposite Guildersfield Road.

Baldry Gardens, 1910. This road is believed to be the widest residential road in Lambeth, mainly due to Mr Alexander Whittet, a former proprietor of the Horns Tavern in Kennington, who lived in a large house called Granville Lodge that stood on the west side of the high road. He complained that the road being laid out opposite his home obstructed the views from his windows towards the Rookery and threatened legal action against the developer unless the road was widened to preserve his outlook.

Barrow Road, 1912. These ancient wooden cottages stood at the western end of Barrow Road until the 1930s when they were swept away and replaced with a large block of flats. Richard Charles Frost lived at No. 44 Barrow Road, and was awarded the Distinguished Flying Medal in 1943 for his 'fine example of keenness, efficiency and devotion to duty' in flying numerous sorties against Rommel's troops in North Africa. The artist Holland Tringham lived at No. 15 briefly during his time in Streatham (see page 97).

Canmore Gardens, 1928. Over 150 children from the surrounding area gathered here in May 1945 for a VE Day street party. The road was decked with bunting and music was relayed along the street through loudspeakers. After the meal the children participated in games and races at the nearby Streatham Vale Sports and Social Club. An unexploded bomb fell near the clubhouse on 17 April 1941.

Colmer Road, c. 1960. This building at the western end of Colmer Road dates from 1869 and is the earliest known example of the work of the local architect Sir Ernest George, who was President of the Royal Institute of British Architects from 1908–10. It was built by Immanuel Church as an infant school. The top of the bell tower was removed in 1970 when the structure became unstable. From the early 1930s the upper part of the building was the headquarters of the 92nd London Company of the Boys' Brigade who were based here for more than fifty years. The hall survives today as the Shree Swaminarayan temple.

Danbrook Road, 1953. The children of Danbrook Road dressed in their party finery gather to celebrate the beginning of a new 'Elizabethan Age' to mark the coronation of Queen Elizabeth II. Helping to distribute the prizes is Cal McCord, resplendent in his stetson hat and Wild West boots. He was the star of a popular post-war radio cowboy show, and lived in nearby Fontaine Road.

Green Lane, 1910. A fine stand of old trees lined Green Lane at the turn of the century when it was no more than a muddy country path leading to Thornton Heath. The lane was lined with thick bushes and it was a brave traveller who journeyed alone along the path to Thornton Heath when darkness fell. This view was taken looking towards Streatham from roughly where the junction with Briar Avenue is today.

Greyhound Lane. The upper picture taken in 1905 shows the small cottages that stood at the top of Greyhound Lane by the High Road. Originally known as Greyhound Place these buildings provided basic accommodation for local residents before they were converted into shops. The house on the extreme right dates from the eighteenth century and was known as the White House, while the more substantial building on the left was built in 1878 and still stands next to the Greyhound public house. The lower view was taken in about 1912 from just south of the junction with Tankerville Road and shows the vista looking up the lane towards Streatham High Road. Allen's grocery stores at 15 Greyhound Lane can be seen on the left. Note the ornate metal railings fixed to the top of the shop sign by the first floor windows. Holland Tringham lived briefly at No. 19 Greyhound Lane (see page 97).

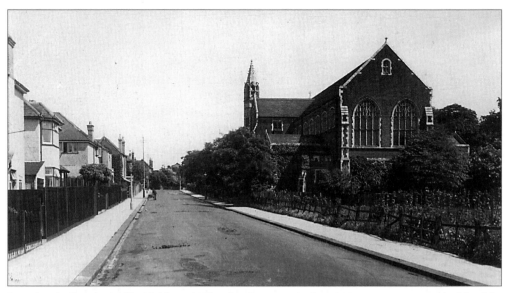

St Andrew's Church, Guildersfield Road. The church was erected in 1889 to commemorate the life of the Revd Stenton Eardley of Immanuel Church (see page 15). The rich red brickwork and terracotta stone dressings made this one of the most beautiful of Streatham's churches. The reredos behind the altar, seen below, was presented to St Andrew's by Sir Ernest George, the local architect who designed the church. It included a mosaic of the Last Supper, with the Ten Commandments carved in two vertical marble panels either side of the altar. The stained glass window above the altar was donated by the congregation in 1918 as a memorial to Mary Cubison, the wife of the first vicar of St Andrew's. The church was gutted by fire in the early hours of 10 March 1992 and was subsequently demolished.

Heathdene Road, c. 1930. Probably Heathdene Road's best-known resident was the actor Deryck Guyler, who gained considerable fame as Mr Potter, the school caretaker, in the hit television comedy show *Please Sir!* He lived here with his in-laws following his marriage to their daughter Paddy in 1941. When his wife's parents emigrated to Canada he took over the house and remained there until 1959 when he moved to Norbury.

Hilldown Road, c. 1930. This road was laid out in 1908 on part of the Streatham Lodge Estate (see page 10). It was originally to be called Welldale Street but this name was changed when plans for the development of the estate were altered to allow for the building of Heathdene Road. The parents of the famous aviator, Sir Alan Cobham, lived at No. 35, and Sir Alan was a frequent visitor here.

Heybridge Avenue. At No. 10 two sisters, Bertha and Julia Munsey, ran Lexden House School for almost half a century. Julia retired as headmistress in 1954 at the grand old age of eighty-five. William 'Bill' Ward, assistant editor of the *Streatham News*, lived at No. 106. He was a keen supporter of many local organizations and was secretary of the Streatham Antiquarian and Natural History Society. Norah Miller, the shop girl turned actress, also lived in this road, and appeared in the film *The Master of Ballantrae* with Errol Flynn in 1952. Plans to develop a greyhound track on land between Baldry Gardens and Heybridge Avenue in 1937 were eventually dropped, much to the relief of local residents. The top photograph was taken in about 1911 and the bottom view dates from about 1925.

Hopton Road, *c.* 1909. Plans for this road were laid out in 1877 when the surrounding land was developed as the Coventry Park estate (see page 19). Originally the stretch of the road leading to Streatham Common North was called Notley Road, but the name was changed to Hopton Road in 1885. At No. 53 lived Henry Aland, who helped cast the statue of Boadicea which stands on the Thames Embankment opposite Big Ben. For many years the Registrar for Births, Deaths and Marriages for Streatham lived at No. 33 Hopton Road. Oscar Grasso, violinist with the Victor Silvester Orchestra also lived in this road, and performed in over 5,000 radio and television shows and on more than 3,000 records. The junior branch of St Helen's School for Girls was based at No. 145. In the picture below the spire of the Streatham Methodist Church can be seen on the skyline.

Kempshott Road, *c.* 1913. This road was named after Kempshott Park at Southampton, the home of the Crooke family (see page 21). William Shears died at No. 23 in 1917 aged ninety-five. As a young engineer he helped build the *Archimedes*, the first screw driven vessel to be constructed on the Thames. He also worked on early railway locomotive engines, riding on the first train to run to Greenwich with open wagons acting as carriages. He was Master of the Armourers' and Brasiers' Company in 1868 and again in 1886.

Madeira Road, 1908. A number of prominent members of the navy have lived in this road. Charles M. Johnson, Chief Inspector of Machinery for the Royal Navy, died here in 1916. Captain Robert Stone, who took charge of the first German ship to be interned in the First World War, also lived here, as did Commander Ferdinand Feilman, who was in charge of a submarine which destroyed a Zeppelin by gunfire off Heligoland in 1916.

Natal Road, *c.* 1907. Originally known as Potter's Lane, this road was renamed Natal Road in 1880. At No. 64 lived Walter Drayson and his wife with their pet collie sheepdog called Prince. It was Prince's loud and persistent barking that warned his master that a German incendiary bomb had landed in their garden during the Zeppelin raid on Streatham on the night of 23/24 September 1916. Prince's timely warning enabled Mr Drayson to extinguish the blaze before it caused any serious damage.

Northanger Road, *c.* 1914. This road dates from 1885. Houses here suffered extensive damage during the Second World War when a V1 flying bomb fell in nearby Buckleigh Road on 3 July 1944. St Margaret's School operated from No. 7 in the opening years of this century, with school fees set at one and a half guineas a term. Immanuel Church School moved from nearby Factory Square to a new school that was built here in 1977 (see pages 11 & 12).

Pathfield Road, *c.* 1914. Among the former well-known residents of this road was the comedy actress Patricia Hayes, who attended the nearby St Andrew's Convent School that was based at Coventry Hall (see page 19). At No. 107 lived Albert Carr, a former Mayor of Wandsworth, after whom Albert Carr Gardens was named. Thomas Murrey of the Scots Guards also lived here and would enthral local residents with tales of his service with the Camel Corps when he was involved in the relief of Khartoum in 1898.

Streatham Vale. A No. 50 motor bus drives down Streatham Vale in 1928. Only a few years earlier this road was no more than a muddy track through the fields leading to Lonesome, a remote area of wasteland on the borders of Streatham and Mitcham. Up to the time of the development of the Streatham Vale Estate, the main inhabitants of the area had been a few nomadic groups of gypsies and the occasional tramp. The area was treated with much caution by the locals and few would journey alone at night beyond Streatham Common station.

Streatham Park cemetery, *c.* 1920. In 1909 seventy acres at Lonesome were laid out as a public cemetery. Once known as the Great Southern Cemetery, it was planned to cater for ⅕ of all burials in south London. Many variety artists have been laid to rest here, including Lizzie Colins who died in 1938 and who was famous for originating the popular music hall song 'Ta-ra-ra-boom-de-ay!' One of the largest funerals in recent times was that of Ronald 'Buster' Edwards, one of the notorious 1963 train robbers, who hanged himself from a girder in his lock-up near his Waterloo flower stall on 28 November 1994. The underworld turned out in large numbers at the cemetery to pay their last respects to a man who became one of the country's best known criminals. In 1932 a public cemetery for Jews was opened here and a crematorium was added in 1936.

Tankerville Road, *c.* 1910. A former resident of this road was William Hunt, who was a member of the royal household for almost fifty years serving three monarchs – Queen Victoria, King Edward VII and King George V. At the time of his retirement he held the post of residential representative in charge of Holyrood Palace in Scotland. The first bombs to fall on Streatham in the Second World War were dropped outside No. 18 Tankerville Road on 7 September 1940, on what is recognized as the first day of the blitz.

Westwell Road was named after a large mansion that stood near this spot which was the home of Andrew Hamilton (1793–1858). He donated the land on which Immanuel Church was built, the tower of which can be seen in this picture taken in about 1907. Alfred Toye lived at No. 7. He was an optician, whose six sons followed in their father's footsteps setting up their own opticians businesses in Streatham, Dagenham, Twickenham, Wembley, Hounslow and Putney. The local artist Holland Tringham resided at No. 22 (see page 97).

STREATHAM COMMON
& THE ROOKERY

This panoramic view of Streatham Common was taken from the bell tower of Immanuel Church, c. 1910. Among the many famous people to have visited the common was the painter Vincent Van Gogh, who made a sketch here in 1874. In a letter to his brother he wrote, 'Enclosed is a little drawing. I made it last Sunday, the morning when my landlady's little daughter died; she was thirteen years old. It is a view of Streatham Common, a large grassy plain with oak trees and gorse. It had been raining overnight; the ground was soaked and the young spring grass was fresh and green. As you see, it is sketched on the title page of Poems by Edmond Roche.' At that time Vincent was lodging in the Kennington home of John Parker, a publican. Sadly the sketch has disappeared and we can only imagine what view greeted Vincent's sad eyes that Sunday morning when he sought solace on the common after the tragic death from pneumonia of young Elizabeth Parker.

Streatham war memorial, c. 1935. The bowed head of the soldier on Streatham's war memorial can be seen through the trees on the corner of Streatham Common South and the High Road. To the right of the statue is a large house called 'The Chimes' which was converted after the First World War into a social club for ex-servicemen. The house was named after a clock on the building that struck the hours and quarters, the chimes of which could be clearly heard across the common.

Cricket on the common, 1910. The sound of leather on willow has been heard on Streatham Common from at least 1806, and probably much earlier. The Streatham Cricket Club played here every week from the second Saturday in May to the last Saturday in August. The club was formed at the Horse and Groom pub in May 1806 and among its rules was that 'Any gentleman playing in coloured jackets, breeches, or pantaloons, shall be fined half a crown (2s. 6d.).'

Streatham Common, 1910. In the top picture a group of three nannies exchange gossip on the park bench at the top of the common, while one of their charges looks on. Note the three different styles of uniform worn by the profession at that time, with the traditional white cap and pinny adorning the nanny on the right. The healthy breeze that sweeps across the top of the common was considered to be most beneficial to young lungs and attracted numerous mothers and nannies with their young charges who came to enjoy the fresh air. The picture below shows a group of young girls blackberrying among the bushes at the top of the common in 1914. Behind them three young boys look on, although it is not clear if their intentions are romantic or they are planning to snatch the young maidens' berries!

Streatham Common South. The upper view shows a gentleman resplendent in his summer straw hat strolling up the horse ride adjacent to Streatham Common South. Horses were often exercised along the ride and it was not unusual to see them galloping up the hill towards the bridle path that still cuts through the woods by the car park at the top of the common. However, since the demise of the local riding stables in Gleneagle Mews horses have become a rare sight on the common. The Gleneagle Riding School was operated by Sandra Carnall, who was the youngest managing director in Britain, when at seventeen years of age she not only managed the school but also a stud farm in Sussex as well as a horse export business. A large steamroller can be glimpsed through the trees in the lower view of Streatham Common South taken in the 1920s.

Streatham Common North. The imposing entrance gates to Park Hill can be seen on the left of the upper photograph taken in 1910. Park Hill is the last surviving example of the grand mansions that were built in Streatham in the nineteenth century. It was designed by John Papworth and erected, *c.* 1835, for William Leaf, a London draper. He died here in July 1874 after which the house was purchased by Henry Tate, the sugar magnate of Tate and Lyle fame. In 1923 the Sisters of the Congregation of the Poor Servants of the Mother of God purchased the house since when it has been known as St Michael's Convent. In the lower picture horses and children queue for a refreshing drink of water at the horse trough and drinking fountain that stood almost opposite Leigham Court Road, *c.* 1906. In the foreground two ladies shield themselves from the summer sun with a parasol while one pushes a perambulator.

The British Home and Hospital for Incurables, Crown Lane. The above view shows the hospital shortly after it was opened by the Princess of Wales on 3 July 1894. The original building was designed by Arthur Cawston and cost £22,660. In 1913 the Queen Alexandra Wing was added to the hospital (seen in the lower aerial photograph taken in the 1920s). Queen Alexander, the former Princess of Wales, was a keen patron of the hospital and each year allotted £500 to the home from the proceeds of the Alexandra Rose Day, in addition to supporting a number of beds and pensioners here. When she died in 1925, the then Duchess of York, the present Queen Mother, became patron of the hospital. She made her most recent visit to the home in June 1996 when she opened the new wing built to commemorate the 100th anniversary of the hospital's move to Streatham.

The Rookery Gardens. A large house called 'The Rookery' stood to the left of the cedar tree seen in the centre of the top photograph taken in about 1926. It was here in the eighteenth century that huge crowds came to drink from the famous Streatham mineral wells. The healing properties of the wells were discovered in a neighbouring field in 1659 when farm labourers weeding there, quenched their thirst at the spring and experienced the purgative qualities of the water. Great claims were made for the beneficial effects of the Streatham waters, which were claimed to cure all manner of ills including rheumatism, gout, jaundice, bilious attacks and even blindness! The strength of the elixir was highly regarded, one cup of which was said to be equivalent to three doses of that from Epsom. By the early 1790s the wells had become contaminated and the business was transferred to a new spring that had been discovered off Valley Road.

The old Rookery building was demolished by the London County Council shortly before they opened the gardens to the public in 1913. The well which marks the location of the original mineral springs can be seen in the top picture taken in about 1938. The photograph below shows the White Garden in 1911. Queen Mary made a number of visits to the Rookery and in October 1936 took those present by surprise when she turned up unannounced with the Princess Royal. It was while the Queen and her daughter were strolling through the old garden by the 'wishing well' that they met the park keeper, Mr W. Purland of Newlands Road, Norbury, who told them briefly of the history of the grounds and the former house, which was the home of Sir Kingsmill and Lady Key (see page 15).

CENTRAL STREATHAM
— THE HIGH ROAD

FROM STREATHAM STATION TO ST LEONARD'S CHURCH

This view of Streatham High Road looking up the hill from Streatham Station Approach was taken in 1912. The lack of traffic suggests that the area had not quite shaken off its rural origins, and this is emphasized by the fact that there is not a single structure in view that was more than thirty years old when this picture was taken. Most of the buildings seen here were erected in the 1880s when Streatham was transformed from a small, sleepy country town into a large London suburb. The rows of impressive shops which lined both sides of the High Road were a source of much pride to the local residents. People journeyed from near and far to shop in Streatham as many local traders were renowned for the variety of their merchandise and the quality of the service they provided.

On the left of the top photograph is the row of shops that formed Station Parade, on the site of which Safeways supermarket was built in 1984. Nos 8 and 8A were the offices of the *Streatham News* and a ladies' tailors, both of which were hit by lightning in August 1905. On the right is Queen's Parade which was erected in 1885. At No. 235 Cpl. B. Hallows lived. He was a Royal Engineer motor cycle despatch rider in the First World War, and was awarded the French Medal for Valour. Next to Queen's Parade, to the right of the tram, is the entrance to the Empire Picture Palace, one of Streatham's earliest cinemas which was opened in 1910. It was built on the site of Jenks' stables which accommodated some forty horses. The old coaches pulled in here to change horses while their passengers refreshed themselves in the adjoining Bedford Park Hotel. The pub was built in 1882 and can be seen next to the cinema, to the left of the tram, in the picture below, *c.* 1913.

The Triangle, 1916. This fine parade of late Victorian shops, at the junction of Streatham High Road and Gleneldon Road, dates from 1885 and was designed by the architect Frederick Wheeler. The name 'TRIANGLE' can still be seen in a terracotta plaque at third floor window-level in the front of the building, directly under the chimney stack. Gadsby's, Streatham's well-known art shop, was located at Nos 326–8 Streatham High Road from 1946 until it closed in 1996.

Streatham Methodist Church at the High Road junction with Stanthorpe Road, *c.* 1910. The foundation stone of the church was laid in May 1882, with services being held here for the first time in the following year. The church steeple was added in 1889 and was a well-known landmark on the High Road until the building was demolished in 1967. The site is now occupied by an Iceland supermarket, however, a clause in the lease prevents them from selling alcohol, a reminder of one of the principles of the previous inhabitants of the site.

Streatham High Road, *c.* 1910. Horse-drawn carts, ready for traders to load their merchandise for delivery to local customers, line the stretch of Streatham High Road leading up the hill towards the green. On the left is Francis and Sons, one of Streatham's largest grocery and provision shops. Some of their wears can be seen displayed outside the store with poultry dangling from a trestle table on the pavement. Note the large gas lamps hanging over the shop windows which were used to illuminate the merchandise in the hours of darkness. The delivery trap of G. Fairbank, fishmongers and poulterers, can be seen in the photograph below which was taken in 1910. This business operated from No. 318 Streatham High Road and was eventually taken over by the Mac Fisheries chain of stores.

Streatham Green, 1807. This sketch by local artist Holland Tringham (see page 97) shows the view across Streatham Green looking towards the ancient cottages that lined the eastern side of the High Road. Called Bedford Row, these buildings were named after the Duke of Bedford, the then Lord of the Manor of Streatham and Tooting Bec. This terrace of small cottages was all there was to Streatham High Road until the road was developed in the 1880s. It must have been quite a culture shock for the old residents of the neighbourhood when, within the space of a few years, their village shopping centre changed from the view seen above to that shown below in 1912. The modern shops, with large plate glass windows with goods displayed from floor to ceiling, are a far cry from the small shuttered windows seen in Tringham's drawing.

Streatham Forge, 1867. Streatham's ancient blacksmith's shop stood on the northern side of Streatham Green between the High Road and Mitcham Lane. For centuries the sound of hammer on anvil echoed through the local streets as the blacksmith plied his trade. The village 'lock-up' can be seen on the right, behind the forge. It was here that local drunks were confined over night until they had sobered up and where petty offenders were imprisoned to contemplate their misdeeds.

The Dip, 1911. One can almost feel for the poor horses straining at their harnesses as they pull their heavy carts up the steep hill to the High Road junction with Mitcham Lane. The hill was so steep that an extra horse was often hired from the nearby blacksmith's shop and attached to the wagons at the bottom of 'the dip' to help over laden carts negotiate the incline. For well burdened transports going down the hill the horse would be hitched to the rear of the cart to help ease the strain on the leading horses.

The Dyce fountain, 1909. The Dyce fountain stood at the junction of Streatham High Road and Mitcham Lane from 1862 to 1933 when it was transferred to Streatham Green. It was erected by parishioners as a tribute to William Dyce, the famous artist who lived locally and who was churchwarden of St Leonard's in 1862. He designed the chancel that was added to the church in 1863. Dyce died on St Valentine's Day 1864 and was buried in St Leonard's graveyard.

St Leonard's church, *c.* 1600. This Holland Tringham drawing shows a representation of what St Leonard's Parish Church is thought to have looked like in the year 1600, although it includes a number of gravestones and tombs that were not erected until the 1800s. The only surviving part of the church is the base of the tower which dates from the mid-fourteenth century. However the church itself has much earlier origins and a chapel existed here prior to the Norman invasion. Income from this chapel was valued at 8*s.* a year in the Domesday survey made in AD1086. St Leonard's has undergone a number of rebuildings over the centuries, the last taking place in 1975 after the church was gutted by fire. Prior to this the church was rebuilt in 1831–2 when the present tower, spire and main body of the church was formed as we see them in the picture below taken in about 1906.

St Leonard's Church, *c*. 1928. A policeman and bus inspector pause to chat by the High Road entrance gate to St Leonard's. The spire of the church was a well-known local landmark, and before tall buildings were erected along the High Road it was clearly visible to travellers journeying along the road to and from London.

STREATHAM VILLAGE

Sunnyhill Road, c. 1912. This road has its roots as an ancient trackway leading from Streatham village to Knight's Hill, a detached part of the parish and of Leigham Court Manor at Norwood. Mention of the route is made in 1547, although it was in existence long before this date. The road that survives today dates from 1867 and gets its name from its location running across the 'Sunny Field' or 'Great Sunny Hill Field' – a small hill off the High Road providing an area of open ground and hence a sunny spot. The road originally comprised six blocks of terraces and cottages. In 1884 the subsidiary names of Leigham Lane, Hillside Terrace, Alpha Villas, Streatham Cottages, Park View Villas and Lyndhurst Villas were abolished and the entire length of the street was renamed Sunnyhill Road.

Dowsett & Jenkins, 3 Sunnyhill Road, *c.* 1910. In the closing years of the nineteenth century Henry Dowsett and Arthur Jenkins opened a builders and decorators business here. Soon afterwards they also operated as funeral directors and this enterprise flourished, the firm eventually becoming one of the largest funeral directors in Streatham. Both men were popular and well-known members of the local community. Mr Dowsett lived for many years at 97 Sunnyhill Road and was a devout baptist, worshipping at the Lewin Road Church for more than fifty years. Mr Jenkins lived a few doors away at 101 Sunnyhill Road and was a lifelong supporter of the Trinity Presbyterian Church in nearby Pendennis Road. Their premises are on the immediate left of the picture below taken in about 1913, looking down Sunnyhill Road.

Sunnyhill Road, *c.* 1907. George Freeman lived at No. 16A until he died in June 1952 aged seventy-four. He was a member of a well-known cricketing family, his father being groundsman and umpire for the Streatham Cricket Club. Although a 'useful bowler', George was never to attain the cricketing heights of his two younger brothers. One was the famous England bowler, Alfred Percy 'Titch' Freeman, who played for Kent from 1914 to 1936. He is widely considered to have been one of the finest right-arm-leg-break, top-spin and googly bowlers of all time. Standing only 5 ft 2 in tall, 'Titch' became the only bowler to take more than 300 wickets in a season. He died at his home 'Dunbowlin' in Bearstead, Kent in 1965. George's other brother, Jack Freeman, played for Essex between 1905 and 1928 and scored 14,507 runs for the club in 577 innings, including 26 centuries.

Curtis Brothers Dairy, Valley Road. These photographs show the variety of milk carts in use at Curtis Brothers Dairy in the First World War, when many women were employed to undertake the milk rounds as the local milkmen volunteered, or were called up, for service in the armed forces. The dairy was founded by Thomas Curtis who moved to the Valley Road farm from Balham in the 1870s. On his death in 1883 his three sons, James, Arthur and George, took over the business and traded as Curtis Brothers Dairies. Work at this time was very hard and the brothers would start their days at 4.30 a.m., never knowing at what time they would finish. Each milkman was expected to milk a number of cows twice daily as well as completing three milk delivery rounds a day. The brothers steadily built up their business and acquired a number of neighbouring dairies (see page 16).

In 1910 Curtis Brothers built a new 'model dairy' at Valley Road incorporating the latest technology available. In 1916 they amalgamated with Messrs Dumbrill's Dairy, and in the following year they merged with United Dairies, James Curtis taking up the post of area director. The dairy continued to flourish as a member of United Dairies and the works were further upgraded. In 1928 delegates attending the World Dairy Congress in England visited the Streatham works which were then considered to be among the finest in the world. Part of the site is still connected with the milk trade and is now operated by Unigate Dairies. The balance of the site has been developed for housing and the original mineral wells building, the old Valley Road farm house, has been restored and now forms part of the residential development.

91 Sunnyhill Road, 1912. This postcard was sent by Ernie Pierce to his cousin, a Mrs Jupp of Henfield in Sussex, on the 31 July 1912. It shows his family home in Sunnyhill Road, in the heart of an area now known as Streatham Village. As was common in the years prior to the First World War ivy is engulfing the front of the house and clematis has been trained round the doorway. Ernie's father, Alfred Pierce, moved here some time after 1910 and was the district secretary for the National Deposit Friendly Society. His eldest son, also called Alfred, tried repeatedly to enlist for active service in the First World War, initially without success, but was eventually accepted by the 16th Middlesex Regiment in 1915. He was quickly promoted to the rank of lance corporal, but sadly was killed at the front in 1916.

MITCHAM LANE

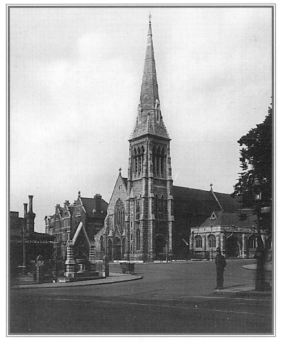

*The Church of the English Martyrs at the junction of Mitcham Lane and Tooting Bec Gardens,
c. 1930. The spire of the Roman Catholic Church of the English Martyrs soars 136 ft 9 in above the
ground. This caused some consternation when it was erected in 1894 as it was 9 ft higher than the spire of
its long standing neighbour, the ancient parish church of St Leonard's. The English Martyrs owes its
existence to the generosity of Robert Measures, who donated the land and contributed a significant sum
towards the building of the church. Although a non-Catholic himself, he was motivated in this gesture by his
wife who was of the faith. The Measure family lived near to the church in a large mansion called Woodlands,
and small sculptured heads of Mr Measures, his wife, and their children
can be seen inside the church.*

The Presbytery and Church of the English Martyrs, *c*. 1907. The ivy-clad presbytery stands on part of a site formerly occupied by three large houses which faced Streatham Green. The Church of the English Martyrs was built on part of the grounds of Russell House, a large eighteenth-century mansion which occupied an extensive plot of land on the corner of Mitcham Lane and Tooting Bec Gardens.

Interior of the Church of the English Martyrs, *c.* 1910. As can be seen in these photographs this church is by far the most ornate in Streatham. Behind the high altar is a magnificent reredos containing a group of the English Martyrs, with a central spire forming a canopy to the throne above the tabernacle. In the tabernacle is a brass crucifix surmounted with a silver triple crown supported by two angels. The Shrine of the Blessed Virgin in the nave (below right), was subsequently dismantled and the statue was placed in the garden of the neighbouring St Mary's Convent. It has since been returned to the church and can now be seen in the Sacred Heart Chapel. Between the windows in the aisles are the fourteen Stations of the Cross, carved in great detail and surrounded with ornate stonework frames.

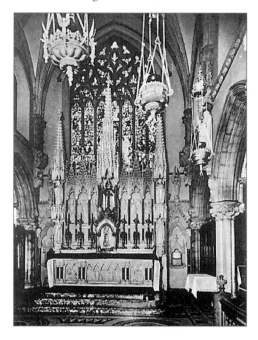

Streatham fire station, *c.* 1916. The pictures above and below left show the old Streatham fire station which was opened in December 1903. The station was one of the first in the country to be fitted with the 'hanging harness' where the horses' tackle was suspended on the front of the escape. When the emergency bell rang, the horses would run out of the station and stand under the harness which would drop down on them and be secured in a matter of seconds by the attendant firemen. Streatham held the divisional record and could turn out in full harness in only twenty-eight seconds. Prior to the opening of the Streatham fire station, the appliances were housed at No. 45 Mitcham Lane and a temporary 'duty hut' on wheels was positioned behind the Dyce fountain at the junction of the High Road and Mitcham Lane as seen bottom right.

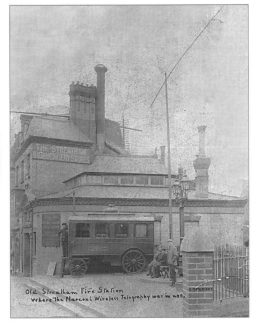

Old Streatham Fire Station
Where the Marconi Wireless Telegraphy was in use.

Mitcham Lane Cottage behind the forge, *c.* 1867. This sketch by Holland Tringham (see page 97) shows the old cottage at the top of Mitcham Lane that was the home of the Viger family. At the bottom of the garden of this property, adjoining Streatham Green, were some old sheds used by Mr Maffey to house his cows. Mr Maffey, who only had one arm, lived in Bedford Row (see page 48) where he ran a small dairy business. He died from injuries he received when attacked by a gang of thieves in Southwark in the 1870s.

Mitcham Lane, *c.* 1922. St Leonard's Girls' School building can be seen on the left. The first parish school was built here in 1838. As the number of children in the area increased it became necessary to provide additional accommodation and the school was rebuilt and enlarged in 1868 and again in 1909. The junior school transferred to new premises further down Mitcham Lane in 1968 with the infants following in 1985.

Thrale Hall, *c.* 1917. This was a large Victorian building occupying an extensive site on the corner of Mitcham Lane and Ambleside Avenue. It was used as a school in the 1860s and was named after the Thrales who lived at Streatham Park in the eighteenth century (see page 71), although contrary to popular belief it had no connection with the family other than being built on part of their estate. The picture below shows an early motorcar in the driveway of the house when it was in use as a residential hotel under the ownership of H. Tuff, who can be seen standing in the doorway. The hotel had a chequered career, and a number of its residents attempted or were successful in committing suicide, although this was not considered a comment on the level of service provided by the establishment. Housing has now been erected on the site.

Two cyclists race a tram down Mitcham Lane in 1914. Note the tall telephone poles standing on the right-hand side of the road that were a common site in Streatham streets up to quite recent times. Mitcham Lane was a very popular residential road and is lined with some fine late Victorian and Edwardian houses which afforded spacious and comfortable accommodation for the aspiring middle classes of the day.

Mitcham Lane, c. 1907. The Streatham Park Hotel, subsequently rebuilt and now known as the Park Tavern, is on the left of this view looking up Mitcham Lane towards Streatham. This pub started life as a beer shop eventually gaining a full licence in 1884 after repeated attempts by its then owner, Henry Harding. Scenes for the £1.6m feature film *Empire State* were shot in the Park Tavern's boxing gym in 1986. The film told the story of London's gangland underworld.

Mitcham Lane Baptist Church. *c.* 1905. The church was designed by George and R.P. Baines and is a Grade II listed building. The foundation stone was laid by Charles Phillips on 23 October 1902 and the building was opened for worship a year later. It cost £5,800 and could accommodate up to 600 people. It is interesting to note that it was equipped with electric lighting, as opposed to gas which illuminated most other churches in Streatham at that time. Andrew Carnegie, the famous millionaire, contributed £200 towards the cost of the organ which was installed in 1910. New halls were built behind the church in Welham Road in 1955 at a cost of £14,000. These drew criticism at the time being considered by some to be too 'modern' in contrast to the more traditional lines of the church. These halls were connected to the church structure in 1967. Note the church spire which was taken down in the 1960s.

St James' Church and church hall. The photograph above shows the temporary church, *c.* 1908. This was erected in Welham Road to accommodate the congregation while money was being raised for the church to be built on Mitcham Lane. This 'temporary' building survives today as the church hall. This can be seen behind St James' Church in the view below which was taken in about 1916. The original funds of £9,000 required for the site, the temporary church building and a small endowment for a vicar, were raised by the parishioners of Immanuel Church as a jubilee thanks offering in 1904. The body of the church, nave, aisle and baptistry were all consecrated by the Bishop of Southwark on 30 March 1912, the chancel and vestries being completed and dedicated in 1916. The adjacent vicarage was dedicated on 26 February 1927.

A liveried driver steers the two well-groomed horses of his landau down the centre of Mitcham Lane while his passenger shields herself from the sun with her parasol. In stark contrast an old work horse, fastened to a rickety cart, feeds from a nosebag while its owner delivers some goods to a nearby house. Note the ornate cast-iron railings on top of the garden walls. Most of these were taken for scrap metal in the Second World War and the sawn off support rods can still be seen on some of the surviving walls today. The picture below shows children gathering at the junction of Mitcham Lane and Kettering Street in the autumn of 1912. The boys to the left of the telegraph pole are holding a pair of stilts and it is probable that the prospect of having a go on them has attracted such a large number of local children.

A No. 10 tram negotiates the turning from Southcroft Road into Mitcham Lane, *c.* 1950. Behind the tram is S. Tray's ironmongery shop which has traded from 249 Mitcham Lane for over seventy years. The business was founded by Henry Tray in 1923, who named the shop after his wife, Sarah, who died in 1965. Henry passed away in 1991, at the grand age of ninety-one, and the business is continued today by his son, Stanley.

Streatham Road. The bridge spanning the River Graveney situated in the centre of this picture marks the boundary between the parishes of Streatham and Mitcham (see page 70). It is on the mid point of the bridge that Mitcham Lane changes its name to Streatham Road. The natural valley formed by the River Graveney is also discernable in this photograph which shows both tram and cyclist taking advantage of the incline.

Roe Bridge, Mitcham Lane, *c.* 1960. These photographs show the various plaques that adorned the old Roe Bridge built in 1906. The bridge is named after Sir Thomas Roe, Master of the Merchant Taylors' Company in 1557 and Lord Mayor of London in 1568. Legend has it that he fell from his horse into the River Graveney at this spot and paid to have a bridge erected here for the safety of future travellers. In 1652 the bridge was rebuilt using funds bequeathed by John Wilford, Master of the Merchant Taylors' Company in 1542, who left money in his will for the maintenance of Mitcham Lane. The above stone commemorates this rebuilding and was incorporated into the bridge when it was reconstructed in 1906, and again when it was rebuilt in 1992. The plaque below signifies the bridge as the boundary between the London County Council (LCC) and Surrey County Council (SCC).

WEST STREATHAM STREETS

The entrance to Streatham Park Estate, 1907. Streatham Park was a magnificent mansion that was home to the Thrale family in the eighteenth century. Henry Thrale and his wife, Hester, entertained the leading personalities of the day here, including Dr Samuel Johnson. The great lexicographer was a frequent visitor between 1766 and 1782 and would often spend the middle part of the week in Streatham. Following the death of Henry in 1781, relations between Hester and the doctor cooled, especially after Hester's marriage to her family's Italian music teacher, Gabriel Piozzi. In 1782 Dr Johnson made his last visit to Streatham. The house was later rented to a number of wealthy tenants, including the prime minister, Lord Shelbourne. By the early 1860s it had become very run down and the estate was sold in 1863, following which the mansion was demolished and the surrounding land sold off for residential development.

Aldrington Road, Streatham Park, 1907. This road was laid out in 1878 and was originally lined with large detached houses. Mrs Dorothy 'Dot' King is a resident here, and in Margaret Thatcher's 1991 resignation honours list was awarded the British Empire Medal for her fifteen years service at Downing Street. Arthur Wates, the co-founder of the Norbury-based building company also lived here, as did Susanna Frazer, who celebrated her 105th birthday at the Radclyffe Old Folks Home in 1978.

Entrance to the Blegborough Road Mission Hall, c. 1910. The hall was opened by Sir Horace Brooks Marshall on 25 September 1902. Sir Horace become Lord Mayor of London in 1918 and lived at the 'Chimes' by Streatham Common (see page 36). The Weslyan Mission operated from this building until 1953 when it transferred its activities to the Methodist church in nearby Riggindale Road.

St John's Church, *c.* 1897. Eardley Road is named in honour of the Revd Eardley, the first vicar of Immanuel Church. St John's was built in 1893 as a mission church of Immanuel and was named after the Revd Eardley's college (see page 15). The site for the church was donated by Cannon Ellison (see page 21) and the chancel was erected in memory of Beriah & Elizabeth Drew by their children (see page 93 & 118).

Bull & Co. offices, 94 Eardley Road, *c.* 1910. Henry Algernon Bull ran his furniture removals business from here in the first quarter of the twentieth century. He offered his clients free estimates with distance being no object as the company had experience of transporting items to Europe and Australia. The building survives today, although the clock and the fire alarm post next to the lamppost have long disappeared.

Eastwood Street, *c.* 1907. A popular resident of this road was 'Telephone Bob', Mr Robert Abethell, who lived at No. 6. It was his proud boast that he laid the first telephone in Streatham which was connected to a house in Leigham Court Road. In the subsequent years he was kept busy connecting houses throughout the area as a consequence of which he was well known to many local residents.

Fayland Avenue, *c.* 1907. St Alban's Church can be seen in this view of Fayland Avenue. It was designed by E.H. Martineau in a Byzantine style and was consecrated on 2 April 1887. The roof was badly damaged in the Second World War, and further destruction was caused by a fire in 1947. As a consequence the church was not reopened until 22 January 1949 being re-dedicated on 11 September 1954. The building was subsequently declared a dangerous structure and was demolished in 1984.

Furzedown Drive, c. 1911. A baker's cart pauses in a deserted Furzedown Drive, opposite Furzedown Lodge, while the baker checks his order book with his young delivery boy. The ivy-clad lodge, seen on the right, was erected in about 1865 and replaced an earlier building that stood on this site. It was designed by the architect James K. Knowles senior (see page 76).

Gracedale Road, c. 1910. Houses were erected in this road between 1907 and 1924. In one of them lived Alfred Mason, who was the fireman of the train on which Sir Winston and Lady Churchill set off on their honeymoon, from Victoria station to Dover, en route to the Riviera. Mr Mason celebrated his golden wedding anniversary here in 1956 having married his wife, Susan, in her home town of Ely on 23 June 1906.

Furzedown House, *c.* 1914. This site has an ancient history and can be traced to an old medieval farmstead called 'Furzden', with the old farm house being situated by the junction of Brookview and Clairview Roads. The farm was leased to various tenants, eventually being rented by the Gray family. Under their stewardship it flourished to become the second most valued agricultural estate in Streatham. In 1793 the farm was acquired by Jacob Yallowley, a wealthy banker, who built Furzedown House as his residence and converted some of the surrounding farm land into a park and paddocks. Alterations to the house, which included the addition of an orangery, were undertaken after the purchase of the property by Philip Flower in 1862, who engaged the architect James K. Knowles snr for this work. The house was purchased by the LCC in 1915 and converted into a teacher training college. It now forms part of Graveney School.

Welford's Farm and Dairy, *c.* 1904. Cows graze contentedly in the grounds of Furzedown House which were used by Welford's Dairy in the early years of this century. The dairy operated from the old Furzedown Park Farm, the buildings of which lay to the west of the house by Rectory Lane, and were originally the stables and servants' accommodation for Furzedown House. Welford established his dairy herd here in the 1880s, and from Furzedown Park Farm supplied produce to a number of shops he owned in Balham, Streatham, Tooting and Wandsworth. The lower picture shows one of his milk delivery carts that operated from his shop at 58 Streatham High Road. Welford's cows had to move to pastures new in 1905 when part of the grounds of Furzedown House were sold and the farm buildings were demolished to make way for Ramsdale Road.

Kettering Street. Children outside W. Wood's newsagents seem unconcerned by the headlines on the placards outside the shop warning of a 'Korean Revolt – Japanese Attacked', 'Big German Liner Sinks in Bremen Harbour' and 'Train Disaster – 80 Dead 100 injured'. For most of the first quarter of this century Frederick William Walker ran this shop. His eldest son, also called Frederick, lied about his age and enlisted in the Queen's Westminster Rifles within a few days of the outbreak of war in 1914. He served in the Somme, Salonika, and Egypt and participated in the capture of Jerusalem, where he was awarded the Military Medal. He won a bar to his MM shortly afterwards for 'a splendid example and devotion to duty'. Sadly he was killed in France only six weeks before the cessation of hostilities. The view below, looking towards the railway line, was taken in about 1908.

Moyser Road, *c.* 1908. These views of the shops in Moyser Road were taken shortly after they were opened in the early 1900s and the young sapling trees had been planted on the pavement. Col. R.J. Findlay OBE lived at No. 2. He served with Lord Roberts in the Boer War and was a member of the Imperial General Staff in France in the First World War, for which service he was made a Knight of the Legion of Honour by the French President. After moving to Moyser Road he became a churchwarden at St Alban's Church (see page 75). Another resident was Harry Antill, who died here in 1941 aged seventy-one. He was the senior partner in the firm of Antill and Squires, a local building company, which erected all the houses in Gracedale Road, one side of Fallsbrook Road, and parts of Moyser Road and Thrale Road. Havergal Girls' School was located at No. 50 Moyser Road.

Parklands Road, *c.* 1908. Amy Barker sent this photograph to her mother in 1908 to show her where she and her husband were living in their new home at No. 15 Parklands Road. The street was laid out in 1906 and was named after a large house of that name which stood on Furzedown Road facing Tooting Graveney Common. Mr Frank Bedford Lovis, one of the founders of Tottenham Hotspur Football Club, died here in 1939.

Pendle Road, *c.* 1923. This was the site of Streatham's most fatal VI flying bomb incident in the Second World War which claimed the lives of twelve residents on 3 August 1944 when Nos 117–123 were destroyed. Local residents held celebrations here in 1953 to mark the Queen's coronation and children in fancy dress paraded to the nearby Rosa Bassett School in Welham Road for an afternoon of games and refreshment. 'Uncle Sandy', a local children's entertainer, was on hand to amuse them with his magic show.

Penwortham Road, 1912. Mr Edwin Durrant celebrated his golden wedding at his home here in 1931. At one time he was the owner of 'The Old Curiosity Shop' in London, immortalized by Charles Dickens. He bought the property as a twenty-first birthday present for his son, Leonard, but sadly his son died of asthma when he was only thirty-six years of age and Mr Durrant then decided to sell the lease.

Penwortham Road School. The boys look very smart in their woodworking aprons in this picture, c. 1910. It is difficult to tell who is enjoying the occasion the most, the boys or their teachers, as there is hardly a smile on the faces of those photographed! The school was built in 1907 and was originally called Mitcham Lane School. Probably the oldest pupil here was ninety-year-old Mary Martin, who attended pottery classes at the Adult Education Institute in the late 1970s.

Penrith Street, *c.* 1907. This road dates from 1897 and was named after the small town in Cumbria of the same name situated eighteen miles south of Carlisle. The third VI flying bomb to fall on Streatham fell at No. 25 Penrith Street on 18 June 1944 causing extensive damage to 1,671 properties in the surrounding area. Charles Cole, the local School Attendance Officer, lived at No. 30 Penrith Street until the mid-1920s.

Pretoria Road, *c.* 1911. The sculptor William Woodington lived at No. 78 in 1909. He helped his father carve the relief of the Battle of the Nile which adorns the base of Nelson's Column in Trafalgar Square. He was also responsible for the four large statues of saints on the dome of St Paul's Cathedral. In 1837 his father carved the giant Coad stone Lion that now guards the southern approach to Westminster Bridge.

Ribblesdale Road, *c*. 1911. William Etherton died here in 1933. His family held a record of 142 years service in the royal household. His grandfather served George IV for twenty-four years; his father was thirty-nine years in royal service; his brother worked for the royal family for thirty-two years and William was employed in the Lord Steward's department for forty-seven years, spanning the reigns of Queen Victoria, King Edward VII and George V.

Thrale Road, *c*. 1907. A horse-drawn bus makes its way down Thrale Road when it was still an unmetalled road. The street was laid out in 1888 and was named after the Thrale family of Streatham Park (see page 71). Thomas O'Donoghue, the editor of *Hansard*, the official daily record of parliamentary debates, and chairman of the House of Commons press gallery, lived here. He was awarded the Order of the British Empire in 1951 for his services to Parliament.

Welham Road, *c.* 1910. This postcard was sent to 'Jack' by an unknown resident of one of the houses here. It was forwarded so that Jack could '. . . see our street as it is with all the planks across the road and the trees at the top of the road. Today they have planted the trees all down our side of the road. . . . All the trees at the end of the street is where they have yet to build.' Building work was still under way here in 1926 when the last house in the road was completed.

Westcote Road, *c.* 1908. This road dates from 1868 and was formerly known as Manor Park Villas, Manor Park Cottages and Oak Villas, but was renamed Westcote Road in 1888 in honour of Lord Westcote, who was said to have been a frequent visitor to the Thrale family home at Streatham Park. A huge bonfire was built here on VE night in 1945 and a street party was held attended by local residents dressed in red, white and blue, to celebrate the end of the war in Europe.

CENTRAL STREATHAM
– THE HIGH ROAD

FROM ST LEONARD'S CHURCH TO STREATHAM HILL

Streatham High Road and Mitcham Lane junction, c. 1905. This is the view that greeted travellers approaching the junction at the turn of the century. In the distance, almost in the centre of Mitcham Lane, can be seen the tower of the lodge to the Manor Park Estate. This was designed by the architect R.L. Roumien in the Italian style. It comprised four bedrooms, two sitting rooms , a kitchen and a scullery. The tower was 70 ft high and on a clear day provided an excellent view of the surrounding countryside as far as Epsom, Highgate and Harrow-on-the-Hill. It was built as the residence of the agent to the Manor Park Estate, the entrance to which was guarded by large gates. In later years the tower was used as an advertizing hoarding and can be seen in many old photographs of the area. The lodge was demolished to make way for the building of the Manor Arms public house in 1925.

The above view shows the Christmas decorations that welcomed those entering Streatham High Road from the junction with Mitcham Lane in 1909. Before the First World War it was common practice for the local shopkeepers and traders to decorate the High Road in this fashion. Much time and effort was put into the display and individual shops would dress their windows in an elaborate manner as part of the festive celebrations. This was done to encourage people to visit Streatham, and many would come from far and near to view the decorations and to do their Christmas shopping in the local stores. The view below shows the same stretch of the High Road after the Christmas decorations had been removed. Note the large trees half way down on the left which marks the site of the front garden of the Shrubbery (see page 87).

The Shrubbery, *c*. 1915. This building was erected in about 1768 and was occupied from 1894 by the Streatham College for Girls. Generations of young women were taught here until the house was demolished in 1933 to make way for a parade of shops. The picture below shows the 'Adam Room' with its ornate fireplace claimed to have been by Robert Adam. This was removed and stored in the crypt of St Leonard's church for safe keeping. However the origins of the fireplace became lost in the passing of the years. In 1965 the Revd Morell Smith discovered the fireplace, at which time it had become separated from its overmantle. He was advised by various experts that it was a nineteenth-century fabrication and of no value so he unfortunately destroyed it. Mystery still surrounds the whereabouts of the ornate overmantle, which may have been by Robert Adam, and if so was worth a considerable sum of money.

Streatham High Road, *c*. 1905. The north wing of Bedford House is behind the row of shops on the left of the High Road. Bedford House dates from about 1739 and was built by a Mr Overman. The property was acquired in 1782 by Daniel Macnamara, agent to the Duke of Bedford, who substantially improved it. This included the building of the two wings, parts of which survive today. The Prince Regent is said to have visited Bedford House on a number of occasions when en route to Brighton.

Streatham police station and Thrale almshouses, *c*. 1912. The building on the left is the second police station to occupy this site on the High Road junction with Shrubbery Road. It was built in 1912 to replace an earlier station erected here in 1865. On the right is one of the Thrale almshouses, built by the children of Henry and Hester Thrale to accommodate four poor widows or single women 'who shall have attained an honest old age in this parish.' In 1930 the building was demolished and eight new almshouses were erected in their place in Poleworth Road.

The White Lion, *c.* 1904. This was without doubt the largest and grandest of all Streatham's public houses when it was rebuilt in 1895. High over the entrance door, hanging over the pavement, was a large metal white lion, clearly seen in the view below taken in about 1912. In 1979 the lion sign was removed and is now kept inside the pub. In 1787 the publican made a rather unusual discovery when he found an abandoned baby girl on the steps of the inn. She was subsequently christened in St Leonard's Church and was given the name Mary Lyon to denote the place where she had been found. It was in a house behind the White Lion that the first school for boys was established in the parish in 1813. It continued to operate from here until a purpose-built school was erected in Mitcham Lane in 1838 (see page 63).

For many years the only clock in the High Road was that hanging outside Otto Mohr's shop, seen here *c.* 1905. Mr Mohr ran a successful watch and clock business from No. 85 and prided himself on the accuracy of his timepieces. In 1909 the overhead pole of a passing tramcar broke free and brought his clock smashing to the ground. In 1912 Mr Mohr ceased to be Streatham's unofficial 'timekeeper' when the King Edward VII memorial clock was placed on Streatham Library (see page 92).

Pratt's Department Store, *c.* 1920. This was the largest shop in Streatham High Road and was founded by George Pratt, a local draper. In 1867 he built Eldon House, seen above, to accommodate his expanding business. The store survived until 1990 when it closed and the building was subsequently demolished. A new row of shops was erected on the site and Lidl Supermarket and Argos commenced trading from here in June 1996.

George Mence Smith, 67 Streatham High Road, *c.* 1913. The staff of this household goods and grocery store stand proudly outside their establishment. The windows are crammed with every type of household requisite imaginable to tempt prospective purchasers into the shop. Articles available include blocks of Gipsy Black Lead Polish, packets of Bird's Custard Powder, and bottles of Little Tower Lemonade. One of the adverts has a novel variation on the well-known nursery rhyme – it reads 'Mary had a little lamb … with lots of HP sauce!'.

The Tate Library. These two views of the High Road show the Tate Library, built in 1890 thanks to the generosity of Sir Henry Tate who lived at Park Hill, Streatham Common North (see page 39). The above view shows the Library, *c.* 1908, while the picture below dates from *c.* 1920 and includes the King Edward VII memorial clock that was placed on the building in 1912. The library was designed by Sidney J.R. Smith, a popular architect who undertook a considerable amount of work for Sir Henry Tate. This included a number of other libraries, including those in Balham, Brixton and West Norwood, as well as the designs for the Tate Gallery, which Sir Henry presented to the nation in 1897. Sidney Smith was also the architect of the Tate Hall in Prentis Road, now used as a synagogue, and St Thomas's Church, Telford Park, which he designed in association with Spencer W. Grant.

These views show the parade of shops that stood between Pratt's Department Store and Becmead Avenue, *c.* 1908. At the High Road junction with Becmead Avenue once stood a large house called 'Towns End', then situated on the outskirts of the old village of Streatham with only a few scattered dwellings and open fields lying beyond. Here lived Beriah Drew, Lord of the Manor of Leigham and one of the largest landowners in the parish (see page 74 & 118). He died in August 1878 at the grand old age of ninety and was buried in St Leonard's graveyard. He left his estate to be divided between his two daughters, Maria Mortimer inheriting the land to the west of Streatham High Road, and Jane Fisher receiving the land to the east. Drewstead Road was named in honour of his family.

The Astoria cinema. The above photograph shows the view looking up the High Road from the junction
with Pendennis Road, *c.* 1910. At that time a number of large detached houses still lined the right-hand
side of the road, as is evident from the large trees standing in their front gardens. Chesterfield House
stood by the junction with Pendennis Road. This was demolished in 1929 to make way for the building of
the Astoria Cinema (below) which opened for business on 30 June 1930. When this photograph was
taken in 1932 *Let Me Explain Dear* starring Gene Gerrard was the main feature with *I Am A Fugitive From A
Chain Gang* promised for screening in the following week. In 1961 the Astoria changed its name to the
Odeon and in 1991 it became the largest Odeon in Greater London and South East England with 1,955
seats and five screens.

Two views of the High Road showing the area around Norfolk House Road. Norfolk House was one of the grandest mansions in the neighbourhood with grounds extending down to Mount Ephraim Lane. Here Christopher Gabriel lived, whose brother, Sir Thomas Gabriel, was Lord Mayor of London in 1866. Following the death of Christopher's widow in 1898 the property was sold and the estate developed for housing. The large block of flats called 'The High', seen below on the right, was erected in the late 1930s. Among the well-known people to have resided here are Shaw Taylor, of television's *Police 5* fame; David Jacobs, the television and radio personality (see page 123); Ross Parker, the songwriter who wrote 'There'll Always be an England'; and Sally Ann Stapleford, British figure ice skating champion.

Leverett & Frye's shop, 111 Streatham High Road, *c.* 1905. Three notices in the window of this well-known Streatham store urge customers to 'Ask Gently but Firmly for Skipper Sardines'. In 1893 a shop assistant sneaked out to a hut at the rear of the premises for a quiet smoke. Unfortunately a spark from his match set light to some straw and within minutes the building was ablaze. Fortunately the other shop assistants helped him quickly extinguish the flames but one can imagine his embarrassment as the fire tenders from Tooting, Clapham, and Brixton arrived on the scene to find the shed a pile of smouldering ashes. The picture below, *c.* 1903, shows a typical delivery cart used by the traders of the day. This was in the employ of Teetgen & Co., tea merchants, operating from 56 Streatham High Road.

The Horse and Groom, 16 Streatham High Road. This sketch by Holland Tringham shows the public house as it was in the 1860s. This was demolished in 1865 to make way for the existing building, currently called 'Big Hand Mo's'. The Horse and Groom was a popular stopping point for coaches on the Brighton Road, where horses would be changed while passengers refreshed themselves at the bar. On one occasion a change of horses was completed here in a breathtaking forty-seven seconds. It was at the Horse and Groom that the Streatham Cricket Club was formed in May 1806 (see page 36).

Holland Tringham was born in Hammersmith on 10 October 1861. He was a talented artist undertaking work for the leading journals of the day, including the *Illustrated London News*. On more than one occasion he painted the portraits of King Edward VII and Queen Alexandra, and was one of the few artists who could boast of having received letters signed personally by the Queen. He moved to Streatham at the height of his career in 1891, living at various addresses, including 15 Barrow Road, 22 Westwell Road and at 19 Greyhound Lane. His parents also lived locally, residing at 6 Baldry Gardens and at 3 Drakefield Road, Balham. With the development of photographic printing at the turn of the twentieth century, his career began to decline and he died under tragic and destitute circumstances at Douglas on the Isle of Man on 26 March 1908 at the age of forty-five. This book features six views of Streatham by him, most of which he based on photographs taken in the 1860s.

Holly Lodge, 29 Streatham High Road, *c.* 1884. This is typical of the row of detached, large, Victorian houses that lined Streatham High Road. Between 1869 and 1884 this was the home of Alfred Coleman and his family, seen below in a photograph taken in the garden of the property in June 1884. Mr Coleman was an eminent dentist, being a surgeon and lecturer at St Bartholomew's Hospital and at the London Dental Hospital School. In 1879 he was elected President of the Odontological Society. When Streatham Park was demolished in 1863 (see page 71), Mr Coleman purchased three mahogany doors from the house and had them incorporated in Holly Lodge. When Holly Lodge was demolished in the early 1930s, Mr Coleman's son, Frank Coleman, claimed the doors and they were presented to the Johnson Society.

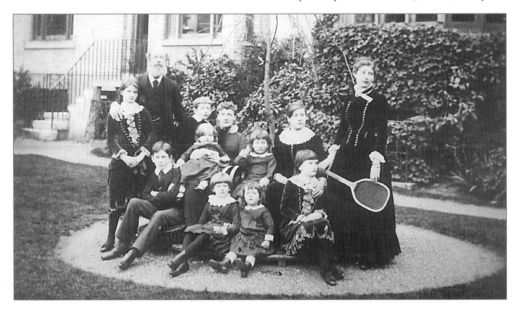

CENTRAL STREATHAM STREETS

Tooting Bec Gardens, c. 1908. This road is lined by some fine, large houses and has always been a popular residential area being ideally situated for both the High Road shops and Tooting Bec Common. Among the former residents here has been Dr Pauline Cutting, who was awarded the OBE in 1987 for her work in the Palestinian refugee camps in war-torn Beirut; Arthur Coaten, the Daily Telegraph's *racing expert, who wrote under the byline 'Watchman' in the 1930s; and the niece of Sir John Barbirolli, the famous conductor, who lived here in the 1960s following her marriage to Timothy Jaggard at the Church of the English Martyrs. A gruesome discovery was made here in June 1911 when the body of George Greenhead, a bricklayer's labourer, was found hanging from the first floor landing of an unfinished house in this road.*

Ambleside Avenue, *c.* 1910. This road was laid out in 1879 when that part of the street from Gleneagle Road to Mitcham Lane was originally known as Inverleith Avenue. However the name was changed to Ambleside Avenue in 1905. The road is best known today as being the home of Cynthia Payne, who was arrested for operating a brothel here for which clients paid for services by using luncheon vouchers they purchased for cash. Her neighbours here were the composer Carl Davis and his wife, the popular television comedy actress of *Bread* fame, Jean Boht.

Becmead Avenue, 1903. At one time all Streatham streets looked similar to this view of the land on which Becmead Avenue was laid out. Dennis Wheatley, the author, lived at 'Friars Croft', No. 1 Becmead Avenue. His family moved here in 1910, when he was thirteen years old, and lived in some comfort, employing a cook, housemaid and a nurse who looked after his younger sister, Muriel. Dennis continued to reside here until 1944 (see pages 110 & 120).

St John the Baptist's Nursery Home, Garrads Road, *c.* 1913. This building has been known by a number of different names including Streatham Grove and more recently Saxoncroft. For many years it was used as a private nursing home and subsequently as a retired persons home owned by Lambeth Council. The picture below shows the dining room of the Grove, *c.* 1907. Garrads Road is named after Robert Garrard, the crown jeweller, who was churchwarden of St Leonard's church in 1850. He lived at Woodfield, a large, impressive mansion situated at the end of this road on a site just north of the Garrads Road junction with Abbotswood Road (see page 107).

Fernwood Avenue, *c.* 1924. Plans for this road were first prepared in 1909. The man who drove the last London tram lived here. He was George Utting who spent most of his life as a tram driver. It was his responsibility to drive London's last tram into the breaker's yard at Charlton in 1952 where it was subsequently broken up. Among his mementoes was the first ticket issued on an electric tram and the very last ticket issued on a London tram.

Prentis Road, *c.* 1911. This road dates from 1903 and was named after the family of Elizabeth Drew, the wife of Beriah Drew, the Lord of the Manor of Leigham (see page 93). The actor Eric Berry lived here. A star of stage and screen, he frequently appeared in the West End and in the USA. He appeared in such films as *The Red Shoes* and acted with well-known film stars such as Rex Harrison and Margaret Leighton.

Moorcroft Road. Much excitement was caused here in 1932 when there was a serious fire at No. 17. Bernard Digby managed to get his wife and children out of the house through clouds of dense smoke and was returning to rescue his fifty year old mother-in-law when she appeared at the back window. Throwing herself from the ledge she landing awkwardly in the yard below, sustaining serious injuries to her head and back.

Pinfold Road, c. 1912. Simon Callow, the actor who appeared in the 1994 film *Four Weddings and a Funeral*, was born here. Another resident was Neville Miller, a past President of the Streatham Cricket Club, of which he was a member for more than seventy years, joining the team in 1893, and captaining the side from 1908–34. He also played cricket for Surrey. He was awarded the Military Cross in the First World War.

Rydal Road, *c*. 1912. Robert Brown, a noted botanist and writer, died in his home here on 26 October 1895. He was born in 1842 and was educated in Scotland. He was the botanist on the British Columbia Expedition in 1863, and took command of the Vancouver expedition in the following year. On his return to Britain he became lecturer in natural history at the School of Arts and at the Herriot Watt College in Edinburgh. From 1879 until his death he was the leader writer for the *Standard*.

Stanthorpe Road, *c*. 1908. Some of the land on which this road was laid out in 1881 was reclaimed with soil from the Lots Road Power Station site in Chelsea. This was purchased to fill in a large lake in the grounds of nearby Bedford House, after which the adjoining Ashlake Road was named. Stanthorpe Road was developed by George Pratt, of local department store fame (see page 90), and was named after his son, Stanley, and his wife's maiden name, Thorpe. Alma Taylor, the first British film star to appear in a 'talkie' film lived here.

STREATHAM HILL

This view of Streatham Hill, by Ardwell Road and Cricklade Avenue, shows the 'old and new' faces of the road in the 1930s. On the right are the large blocks of Edwardian shops and flats erected on the grounds of Leigham Court House in the closing years of the nineteenth century. The blocks comprise rich, red brickwork, and incorporate ornate windows on the roof line and rounded turrets at the ends of the Streatham Hill frontages. On the left is Streatham Hill Theatre. Opened in 1929, it was designed with the straight lines and comparative simplicity of style that was common for the period. This is a design philosophy in stark contrast to that adopted by most late Victorian and Edwardian architects and heralds the coming of a new, modern age for post-First World War Britain. The development of the western side of Streatham Hill, with the building of the Gaumont Cinema, the Locarno dance hall and the theatre established Streatham as a major entertainment centre in south London whereas previously it had been regarded mainly as a residential area.

Streatham Hill station, *c.* 1924. The earliest major building erected on Streatham Hill after the First World War was the block of shops and flats at the junction of Sternhold Avenue seen above. These were built on the site of a large house, which was destroyed by bombs dropped in the Zeppelin raid on Streatham on the evening of 24 September 1916.

Gardner's grocery stores, *c.* 1912. This shop stood opposite Streatham Hill station, occupying a row of single storey shops built over the railway bridge near the junction with Leigham Court Road. Mr Gardner's health deteriorated as a result of strains caused by the First World War, which led him to hang himself in 1920. In 1952 Patrick Galvani opened the first Premier supermarket on this site, which was the earliest supermarket chain to operate in Britain.

The ABCD Estate, Streatham Hill, *c.* 1910. The Artisans' Labourers and General Dwelling Company purchased Leigham Court House and grounds in 1890 and laid out an estate of houses on the site. As the residential roads ran in alphabetical order – Amesbury, Barcombe, Cricklade and Downton Avenues – it became known locally as the ABCD Estate. The development began with the erection of the buildings fronting on to Streatham Hill seen here. Shop units were built at street level with rented accommodation available on the upper three storeys. The prospect of large numbers of houses for the upper working class being erected on the estate caused considerable concern to local residents, particularly those living in the large Georgian and Victorian houses that were then situated along Streatham Hill.

Gaumont Palace Cinema, c. 1946. This was opened in March 1932, almost two years after the Astoria. The building was designed on a grand scale by Charles Nicholas and J.E. Dixon-Spain. The portico and entrance hall is 60 ft long and 34 ft deep, and provided access to a grand staircase leading to the Balcony Lounge and Café and to the stalls' waiting foyer, measuring 70 ft long by 23 ft wide. It was converted into Europe's largest bowling alley in 1961 and is now named the Megabowl.

Streatham Hill Theatre, c. 1958. Paul Schofield was appearing at this theatre in *Ring Round The Moon* when this photograph was taken. Streatham Hill Theatre was one of the largest outside the West End of London and was opened in 1929. Among the stage hands working here was Mr Livingstone who lived in Shrubbery Road, Streatham. His son, Ken Livingstone, was the last leader of the Greater London Council and is currently MP for Brent East. The theatre building is now used as a bingo hall and social club.

35 Streatham Hill, *c.* 1932. Typical of the large houses that lined Streatham Hill was this Georgian mansion erected in 1823. It was occupied by Streatham Hill College from 1895 until it was demolished in 1936. In 1840 Charles Few, a solicitor, lived here. His son, Charles junior, married Jane Garrard, the daughter of Robert Garrard, the crown jeweller (see page 101). Charles Few, his wife Jane, and Robert Garrard are all buried in the Garrard family tomb in the parish graveyard at St Leonard's Church, Streatham.

39 Streatham Hill, *c.* 1890. Wooton Lodge was built in about 1823. From 1834 to 1903 it was the home of the Hedges family. William Hedges was a partner in the firm of Hedges & Butler, wine merchants, whose origins dated back to 1667. The business traded from premises in Regent Street. The house was named after the ancestral birthplace of the Hedges family, Wooton in Oxfordshire. The house was demolished in the early 1930s to make way for Wavertree Court.

Telford Avenue tram depot, *c.* 1905. On the right of the tram is the depot that was established here in 1891–2. A winding engine was installed in 1898 to pull the trams up Brixton Hill by means of a continuous steel cable which ran through a covered channel in the roadway. The depot was enlarged in 1904–6 when the system was electrified, and was further extended in 1911. When trams were withdrawn in 1951 the depot was closed and Brixton bus garage was erected on the site.

Tram repair shed, *c.* 1950. Built in 1923 this building survives today as the Stratstone Garage. It was built on the site of Aspen House, the home of the Roupell family. The family developed the nearby Roupell Park Estate. William Roupell was MP for Lambeth, but brought disgrace on his family when he was jailed for forgery. A later resident of the house was William Yeates Baker, the maternal grandfather of the author Dennis Wheatley (see pages 100 & 120).

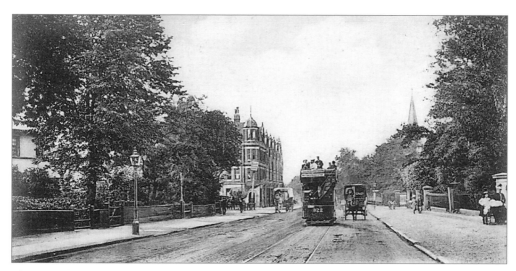

The spire of Streatham Hill Congregational Church can be seen towering above the trees on the right of these photographs, *c.* 1906. Although Streatham Hill becomes Brixton Hill at the junction with Streatham Place and Christchurch Road, the old Streatham parish boundary was situated further along Brixton Hill and ran along Mill Lane (now Morrish Road). The Crown and Sceptre public house can be seen on the left in the picture below. It has stood on this spot since 1822 and may have been named to commemorate King George IV's accession to the throne in 1820. James Arnold, the inn's first host, boasted that fifty coaches to and from the City and West End called at the inn each day. Glen Cornick, a founder member of the well-known pop group Jethro Tull, was the son of the licensee who ran the pub in the 1970s.

Streatham Hill Congregational Church, *c.* 1908. A Union Chapel was erected here in 1829 for the use of a group of Anglicans and Nonconformists. In 1837 the Anglicans left to form the congregation of Christchurch (see page 114) and in 1840 the Baptists moved to the Salem Chapel, in New Park Road. The small Union Chapel was rebuilt in 1871 as Streatham Hill Congregational Church at a cost of £7,836. This building was demolished in 1982 and the new Brixton United Reform Church opened for worship here ten years later in 1993.

STREATHAM HILL STREETS

Granville Lodge, 10 Palace Road, 1902. Thomas Horn and his wife stand proudly outside their home in Palace Road. This impressive three storeyed house was situated on the southern side of the road, opposite the junction with Christchurch Road. The Horn's home was a small building compared with some of its neighbours, and many of the large, detached residences that were built in other parts of Streatham Hill. The coming of the railway to Streatham Hill in 1856 brought the City of London within easy commuting distance of Streatham. The locality's then rural surroundings made it an attractive place for wealthy merchants and city workers to live. To help meet the increasing demand for high quality housing, Leigham Court Road was developed with large detached mansions. The Telford Park Estate, comprising roads of large terraced houses, was subsequently laid out to cater for the aspiring middle classes who were keen to obtain more affordable accommodation in the area (see page 123).

Christchurch, Christchurch Road, Streatham Hill, *c.* 1906. The church was designed in the Byzantine style by James William Wild, and the foundation stone was laid by Archdeacon Wilberforce (the son of William Wilberforce the famous anti-slavery campaigner) on 11 August 1840. Widely considered to be the jewel among Streatham's churches, this is a Grade I listed building. The bell tower is 113 ft tall and is a well-known landmark on the South Circular Road. The church was damaged by a bomb in 1940 and repairs were not completed until 1951. To the left of the church is Christchurch School which was built in 1844. The school quickly established high standards and was well-known for the quality of its teaching. In 1863 Her Majesty's Inspector of Schools reported that the infants school was the best he had ever visited. The photograph below shows Class IV of the school in 1913.

Christchurch Road, *c.* 1908. In a small flat at No. 36 lived Donald McGill, the famous comic postcard artist. Every year millions of his cards were posted to friends and relatives by people visiting the seaside. Despite a number of prosecutions, McGill continued to draw his popular 'saucy postcards' up to the time of his death in 1962 when he was eighty-seven. He was buried at Streatham Park cemetery (see page 33). Today his cards are collectors' items and his original drawings sell for large sums of money.

Hailsham Avenue, *c.* 1910. Although this road was laid out in 1891 houses were not erected for some years. Among its former residents was Jack Short who was captured by the Japanese in the Second World War. During his 3½ years as a prisoner of war he was forced to work on the notorious 'Death Railway' in Thailand. However he was fortunate to survive this gruesome experience and returned safely home in 1945.

Hillside Road, *c.* 1914. Freddie Weyer, commonly known in the 1970s as London's 'Mr Arts', lived here. Mr Weyer was one of Streatham's members on the Greater London Council and was chairman of the GLC's Arts Committee, with responsibility for allocating £3m to arts organizations each year. Mrs Donald Campbell lived at No. 2 from 1909–38. She was a member of the temperance movement and founded the nearby Hitherfield Road Baptist Church in Streatham and the West Norwood Crèche in Hannen Road.

St Simon & St Jude Roman Catholic Church, *c.* 1910. This church was designed by Clement Jackson and was erected in Hillside Road in 1906. The building was soon too small to accommodate its growing congregation and it was extended in 1937 when a new sanctuary was built. After an attempt to purchase Roupell Park Methodist Church failed in 1964 additional extensions to the church were undertaken

Leigham Court Road. The top view dates from *c.* 1904 while the photograph below was taken in about 1912. Leigham Court Road was one of Streatham's premier residential roads and among the important people who have resided here are Sir Arnold White, Queen Victoria's solicitor; George and Joseph Trollope, members of the building firm now known as Trollope and Colls; Frederick Palmer, publisher of the *Church Times*; Dr Arthur Oxley, doctor to Princess Beatrice; William Axtens, partner of Quin and Axtens the famous Brixton department store; George Higgins, partner in the Peckham department store of Jones and Higgins; Sir Frederick Hall, MP for Dulwich; Thomas Wilkinson, President of the Magdalene Hospital; William Saunders, MP and newspaper proprietor; and Charles Robertson, State Page to Queen Victoria.

St Peter's Church, Leigham Court Road, *c.* 1907. Local parishioners first gathered in St Peter's Church for worship in 1870. The building was designed by Richard W. Drew, grandson of Beriah Drew (see pages 74 & 93). In 1886–7 the west part of the nave and a baptistery were added, but only after three sets of plans had been prepared and submitted by the architect G.H. Fellowes Prynne. A new William Hall organ was installed at St Peter's in 1903, which was widely considered to be the best instrument of its type in south London. To mark its 125th anniversary in 1995, the church embarked upon the first stage of an ambitious £200,000 refurbishment programme, with work being undertaken on the roof and stonework of the building. The church is a Grade II listed building.

Lydhurst Avenue, *c.* 1918. This road was laid out on the Leigham Court Estate in 1891 to link Faygate and Hitherfield Roads, although houses were not erected here until a much later date. Note how the ivy creeping over the front of the house on the right has been carefully trimmed back around the road name plate so that strangers to the area would be aware of where they were.

New Park Road, *c.* 1905. Originally known as Balams Lane, this is one of Streatham's ancient trackways that led to the once small hamlet of Balham. Local tradition has it that the great Italian composer Verdi lived at No. 138 during one of his visits to London. Two noted water-colour artists also dwelt in this road. At No. 82 David Cox junior resided from 1860–76, and William Bennett inhabited two houses here, Bleak Hill Villa, and afterwards Milford Lodge, where he died in 1871.

Palace Road, *c.* 1908. This road takes its name from the Crystal Palace which was clearly visible from here. The popular television and radio comedy actress June Whitfield lived in this road as a child. Commander Bill Boakes, a stalwart Parliamentary by-election candidate and road safety campaigner was also a resident here. Between 1951 and 1982 he fought a record thirty by-elections and lost his deposit on every occasion. The author Dennis Wheatley spent his early childhood years at Clinton House, No. 1 Palace Road (see pages 100 & 110). Benjamin Moss lived at Meadowside, No. 20. He was the manager of the *London Journal* whose printing works were located behind his house. The junior department of the Streatham Hill and Clapham High School for Girls was located at No. 28 until 1993 (see pages 126 & 127). William Hughes, general manager of the Prudential Insurance Company, lived at Nos 60–2 from 1884 to the 1920s.

Sternhold Avenue, c. 1914. This road was planned in 1877 and the houses have been renumbered here on several occasions as new properties were built along its length. In July 1952 the Queen Mother came here as part of a tour organized by the London Gardens Society. She visited the prefab home of Mr & Mrs Atkinson who provided her with a conducted tour of their garden. Arthur Bailey, chief warder of the British Museum lived in this road. He joined the museum in 1935, after twenty-six years with the river police, on retirement from which he was presented with the King George V Jubilee Medal. In 1954 he was awarded the British Empire Medal for his services to the museum. The photograph below, taken in 1905, shows the houses that stood opposite Thornton Avenue, the right-hand section of which survives today as a veterinary surgery with new houses erected on the remainder of the site.

Streatham Place. In the top view, taken in about 1908, the yard of Arthur Phelps can be seen on the left. Arthur moved to Streatham in 1883 and took over the builders business that was based at No. 5 Palace Road, which had been established in the area since 1820. He was a staunch Congressionalist and attended the Streatham Hill Congregational Church for over thirty years, where he was a Sunday school teacher (see page 112). Fred Appleby (1878–1956) operated a dental practice at No. 29. He holds the world record for the longest standing track record of all time – it stood for 35 years and 39 days, not being surpassed until 1937. He ran a 15 mile race in 1 hour 20 mins 4.6 secs on 21 July 1902. He ran in the marathon for Britain in the 1908 Olympics but was forced to drop out of the race after 20 miles with blistered feet

Telford Avenue, c. 1906. The tram depot on Streatham Hill can be seen centre left in the top view (see page 110). Telford Avenue was the main thoroughfare of the Telford Park Estate which was developed between 1878 and 1882 by Sutton and Dudley, builders. David Jacobs, the popular television and radio personality who hosted the BBC Television show *Juke Box Jury* was born at No. 24 Telford Avenue, later renumbered No. 42. In recalling his boyhood in Telford Park he often tells of the times that the comedian Bud Flanagan, of The Crazy Gang, gave him lifts to school in his car. Living here in 1963 was Jane Jackson who worked as a sculptor for Madame Tussaud's Waxwork Museum, and prepared the bust of Angus Ogilvy which went on display at the time of his marriage to Princess Alexandra in April 1963.

Tenham Avenue, *c.* 1908. This road dates from 1881. James Barr lived here. He was choirmaster at Westminster Abbey for twenty-eight years, and also at St Thomas' Church, Telford Avenue, Streatham, for seventeen years. Another resident was Detective Sergeant Richard Green who was Princess Margaret's personal detective and travelled with her on all her official visits. Ill health forced him to relinquish his post, and while he was convalescing the Princess visited him to wish him well. He died in May 1950 at the age of thirty-six

Thornton Avenue, *c.* 1904. Formerly known as Thornton Road, the name was changed to Thornton Avenue in 1884. Dr Stanley Roper CVO, organist for more than fifty years at the Chapel Royal, St James's Palace, Buckingham Palace and Queen's Chapel, Marlborough Gate, lived here. He began his career as sub-organist in 1902. He played the organ in Westminster Abbey during the funeral service for the unknown warrior on Remembrance Day, 11 November 1920.

Tierney Road, *c.* 1906. This road came into existence in 1878 and it contains some fine late Victorian terraced houses. Five of these near Streatham Place were demolished when a VI flying bomb fell here on 9 August 1944. Many of the surrounding properties suffered blast damage including some as far away as Montrell, Sulina and Christchurch Roads. Sarah Ann Martin lived at No. 13. She gave her approval for the sale of land held by her family off Garratt Lane, Tooting, on which Streatham cemetery was laid out in August 1891.

Wyatt Park Road, *c.* 1924. Plans for this road were approved in 1906. Mr Beale Gunner, who made Queen Mary's and Queen Elizabeth's (the Queen Mother) coronation fans lived at No. 75. He had the distinction of being the only fan-maker in the Fan Makers' Company at the time of their coronations. Another resident of this road was Norman Preston, editor of *Wisden's Almanac*, the annual cricket encyclopedia, as well as cricket and football editor with the Press Association.

Wavertree Road, *c.* 1910. Plans for this road were detailed in 1883. Elizabeth Legge celebrated her 104th birthday here in April 1984. As a young woman she was a keen suffragette and worked with the Pankhurst sisters in their campaign to get the government to give women the right to vote. Elizabeth was often to be seen in Oxford Street where she would sell the suffragette newspaper. She married a captain in the merchant navy and went with him when he took his ship up the Yangtse River in China. At each port of call she would buy an ornamental plate and this collection adorned the wall of her house in Wavertree Road. Walter T. Dunn, secretary of the Institution of Gas Engineers, also lived here and the Misses Gilson ran Somerville School for Girls at No. 12. The Streatham Hill High School for Girls (later to become the Streatham Hill and Clapham High School for Girls) moved to their new premises here in 1895 (below).

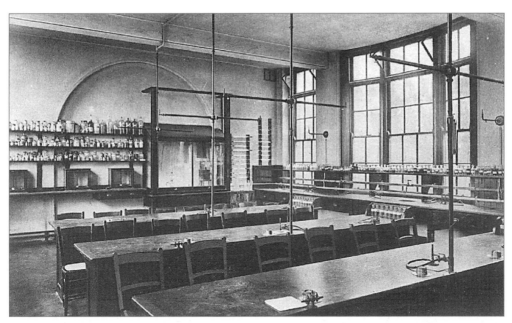

Streatham Hill and Clapham High School for Girls, Wavertree Road. The new school building was opened in February 1895 by the Marchioness of Lorne. The school cost £10,000 to build and provided comfortable, spacious accommodation which offered its pupils every modern facility. The upper view shows the school's well stocked chemical laboratory, while the photograph below shows the wood-panelled library. The school celebrated its centenary in 1987 by holding a special service in Westminster Abbey attended by Princess Alice, Duchess of Gloucester. In January 1994 the senior school moved from here to a new site in Abbotswood Road, by Tooting Bec Common, and the junior school took over the Wavertree Road building.

A Streatham beauty bids you a warm welcome to her suburb in 1911.